Taylor Swift

THE Story of Me

By Riley Brooks

SCHOLASTIC INC.

ISBN 978-0-545-48860-0

12 11 10 9 8 7 6 5 4 3 2 1   12 13 14 15 16 17/0

Book design by Becky James
Printed in the U.S.A.
First printing, September 2012

40

Table of Contents

Introduction

These days just about everyone has heard of super talented singer and songwriter Taylor Swift. The country and pop music superstar has won six Grammy awards, sold over twenty million albums, and gets to go to the biggest award shows for music, television, and movies.

She's been on the cover of magazines, performed for sold-out crowds, and is friends with some of the coolest celebs in Hollywood. But don't let all of her fame fool you—Taylor is still the sweet, down-to-earth farm girl she's always been.

= CHAPTER 1 =
Nashville Dreamer

Taylor Swift was born on December 13, 1989, and grew up in the small town of Wyomissing, Pennsylvania. When she was eleven, Taylor recorded her first demo CD and headed down to Nashville to shop it around. No one was interested at the time, but Taylor didn't give up.

When she was thirteen, Taylor's family moved to Nashville to support Taylor's dream. After three years, Taylor received a record deal with Big Machine Records. She got right to work on her self-titled debut album. When *Taylor Swift* was released in October 2006, it went platinum in just under a year. *Taylor Swift* went on to hit number one on the country charts and it eventually went five times platinum.

Two years later, Taylor recorded her second album, *Fearless*, which hit store shelves on November 11, 2008. It instantly went to number one and went platinum soon after.

By the end of 2009, Taylor was selling out huge arenas on her *Fearless* tour. Her songs were played more than any other artist's for the entire year on the radio *and* streamed the most online! Most artists hope to have that type of success in their entire career, but Taylor was just getting started!

After her *Fearless* tour wrapped up at the end of 2009, Taylor was eager to get back into the studio and record a new album called *Speak Now*—and she had a lot of new material! "When I put out an album, I'd like to think that when people listen to that album it's like a diary of what I've been through in the last two years," Taylor told MTV.com. "So it's a really fun way to express how I feel and what I'm going through." For Taylor, *Speak Now* was about just that: speaking her mind, whether it was about relationships, the media, or even other celebs!

One of the most popular songs from the album, "Mean," is about music critics and other negative voices who have tried to bring

Taylor down. Taylor has admitted that "Back to December" is her first apology song, and fans believe that it is directed at Taylor Lautner, whom she dated briefly. Taylor has written several other songs about past boyfriends, like "Dear John" and "Better than Revenge."

Another song, "Innocent," was Taylor's response to an incident at the MTV Video

Music Awards in 2009 when Kanye West interrupted her acceptance speech for "Best Female Video." Taylor handled the whole incident with grace and she forgave Kanye right away, but her song reveals that the incident stuck with her.

It must have felt great for Taylor to let her feelings be known, and her fans couldn't wait to get their hands on the new album! *Speak Now* debuted at number one on October 25, 2010, and has gone on to be certified quadruple platinum, meaning it's sold over four million copies in the U.S. alone! Taylor went on tour for almost all of 2011 and into 2012 to promote the album, delighting fans around the world.

= CHAPTER 3 =
Taylor Times Four

As much as Taylor's fans love her first three albums, they always want more! Luckily for them, Taylor's fourth album will be released in 2012. Staying true to herself, Taylor has written new songs about her real life experiences, but this album will have a different tone than her mostly upbeat previous records.

Taylor herself has admitted that a lot of the songs on the album are sad. "There's just been this earth-shattering, not recent, but absolute crash-and-burn heartbreak," she told *Vogue*, "and that will turn out to be what the next album is about. The only way that I can feel better about myself—pull myself out of that awful pain of losing someone—is writing songs about it to get some sort of clarity." No one likes to go through heartbreak, but her fans are certain that even her sad songs will be big wins for their favorite country superstar!

CHAPTER 4

Award-Winning Success

Taylor has been winning awards since her first album hit store shelves, and they've only gotten bigger over the years! In 2007, she won her very first award—the Country Music Television "Breakthrough Video of the Year" Award. Taylor told *The Tennessean*, "I can't explain the feeling. I had never been nominated for anything before. I had won nothing before, literally nothing. . . ." She finished off the year by winning the Horizon Award for the best new country singer at the Country Music Association Awards.

In 2008, Taylor won "Top New Female Vocalist" at the Academy of Country Music Awards, "Favorite Female Country Artist"

at the American Music Awards, two CMT Awards, and "Favorite Breakout Artist" at the Teen Choice Awards.

The next year was even bigger. In 2009, Taylor won two Academy of Country Music Awards and two CMT Music Awards. She also won "Favorite Female Album" at the Teen Choice Awards and "Best Female Video" at the MTV Video Music Awards.

By the end of 2009, Taylor set the record for the most songs on the Billboard Top 100 by a female artist at the same time, and she had had the most Top 40 singles for a female artist for the entire decade!

But the high point of 2009 for Taylor was winning the coveted "Entertainer of the Year" award at the Country Music Association Awards—she was the youngest artist in history to win the prestigious award.

Taylor then shook up the music industry

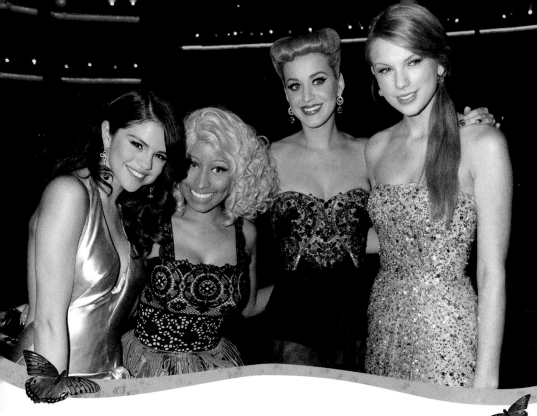

in 2010 when she was nominated for eight
Grammy Awards and won four of them,
including the award for "Album of the Year."
At the American Music Awards she took home
"Favorite Country Female Artist," and won the
"Hal David Starlight Award" from the
Songwriters Hall of Fame. She also won four
Teen Choice Awards and two Nickelodeon
Kids' Choice Awards that year. That's a lot
of trophies!

In 2011, Taylor won two Academy of Country Music Awards, three American Music Awards, and one CMT Music Award. She also won the People's Choice Award for "Favorite Female Artist," and six Teen Choice Awards.

But Taylor's biggest win of 2011 was her second "Entertainer of the Year" from the Country Music Association. Taylor is the second woman in history to win that award more than once! "To win it twice is . . . the coolest thing ever happening to me twice!" Taylor told RadarOnline. Winning that award twice in four years was a really big deal for Taylor!

The year 2012 started with a bang for Taylor when she won "Entertainer of the Year" from the Academy of Country Music. She also won two Grammy Awards and a People's Choice Award for "Favorite Country Artist." And all that was only the beginning of 2012! She's sure to rack up many more nominations and wins as the year continues.

Taylor has won numerous other awards around the globe, including some from Thailand, Britain, Canada, and Australia. It's hard to believe that Taylor is only in her twenties with that many awards on her mantel, but Taylor loves what she does and that definitely shines through when it comes time to give out awards!

CHAPTER 5

Acting Bug

Taylor is well known for her musical talent, but she's also a great actress! In 2008, Taylor appeared in music videos for fellow country stars Brad Paisley and Kellie Pickler. She also filmed a show for MTV called "Once Upon a Prom." In the show, Taylor picked one lucky high school boy, traveled to his town, and went to his prom with him! Taylor made cameos in a few of her friends' movies, like *Hannah Montana: The Movie* with Miley Cyrus, and *Jonas Brothers: The 3D Concert Experience.*

In 2009, Taylor guest starred on CBS's *CSI: Crime Scene Investigation* and had the chance to shine on her own. Taylor's fans were amazed to see just what a great actress Taylor really is! The following year, Taylor's friend Justin Bieber would appear in a CSI episode.

Folks in the acting industry certainly took notice of Taylor's skills. She was asked to host *Saturday Night Live* in November 2009. Taylor dove right into the experience and impressed the show's writers and cast. Taylor's show was one of the highest-rated *SNL* episodes of the entire season!

Finally, Taylor made her way to the silver screen with a small role in the 2010 romantic comedy film *Valentine's Day*. She played a peppy high school cheerleader named Felicia, opposite Twilight saga cutie Taylor Lautner. She had a great time filming that movie, and the icing on the cake was that she won the 2010 Teen Choice Award for "Movie Breakout Female" for her performance!

By that point, Taylor had definitely been bitten by the acting bug. She started reviewing scripts with her agent, looking for a role that she could really shine in. She starred in her first

animated film by providing the voice of Audrey in *The Lorax,* a 3D animated film based on the classic Dr. Seuss book about protecting the environment. Her costars included Zac Efron, Danny DeVito, and Betty White. Recording her part was really fun for Taylor and allowed her goofy side to take center stage. It premiered in theatres in March 2012 and was a huge hit with Taylor's younger fans and their parents.

Hopefully it will be the first of many fantastic lead movie roles for Taylor!

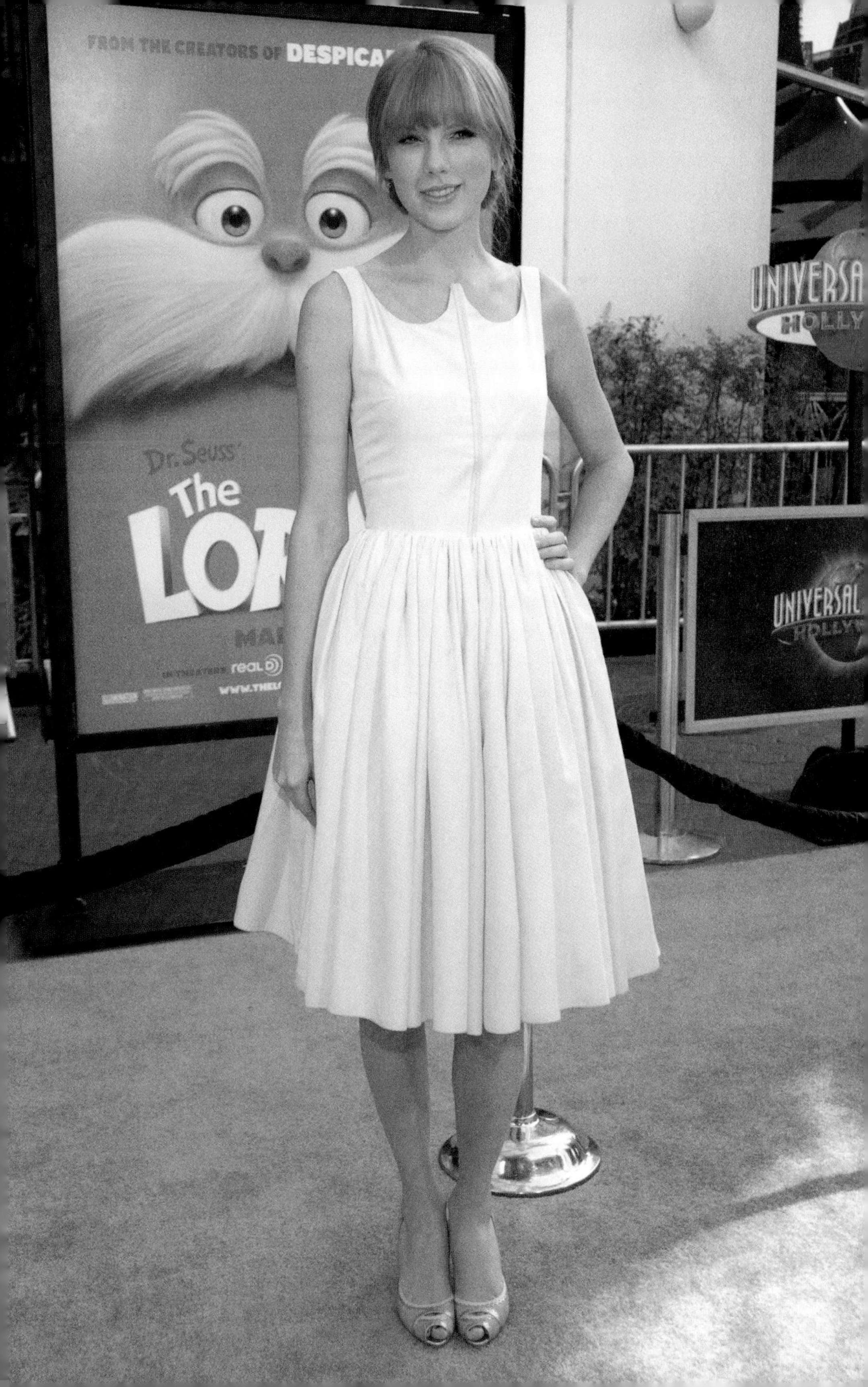
FROM THE CREATORS OF
Dr. Seuss'
The
UNIVERSAL

CHAPTER 6
Fashionably Taylor

Taylor took the world by storm wearing sundresses, cowboy boots, and faded jeans, and, while she still loves those basics, her style has grown up just like she has. These days, you can find Taylor sporting looks by trendy designers like Jenny Packham, Rodarte, and Alexander Wang. Taylor has made appearances at plenty of runway shows, and designers are lining up to dress her.

She has also graced the covers and pages of fashion magazines like *Elle*, *Marie Claire*, *Glamour*, *Teen Vogue*, and *Vogue*. Taylor loves doing photo shoots for magazines, since she gets to wear the latest in fashion and try out new makeup and hair trends in the process.

For her concerts and events, Taylor loves dresses with sequins, and glitzy fabrics that look great under the bright lights and in photographs. For the red carpet, she tends to go with long, elegant gowns—choosing brighter colors or neutrals with shine. She prefers strapless numbers or column gowns with one shoulder that highlight her height. But in her spare time, Taylor sticks to comfortable basics that travel well, since she's always on the road.

Taylor is currently working with the fashion brand L.E.I. to create clothes her fans can buy inspired by her favorite looks. The line features pretty cotton dresses, ruffled tank tops, jeans, and cute cardigans that can be mixed and matched for tons of looks! She loves seeing fans rocking her looks and she hopes to continue working with stylish designers and brands in the future.

= CHAPTER 7 =
Cover Girl

Taylor's fans have always known just how beautiful she is, so they were thrilled to see Taylor working with two world-renowned beauty companies. Elizabeth Arden partnered with Taylor to release her very first perfume, called "Wonderstruck," in 2011. "I love having my fragrance, Wonderstruck, out. It turned out to be something I wear all the time, and I'm so proud of how well it's done," Taylor told *Seventeen*. Taylor can afford to buy any perfume she wants, so the fact that she wears her own shows just how delicious it smells!

CoverGirl Cosmetics has also teamed up with Taylor. In a press release, the general manager of CoverGirl said, "Taylor's naturally polished and beautiful look fits perfectly with the new luxury makeup line [NatureLuxe]." CoverGirl is Taylor's makeup of choice, whether she's going for a fresh-faced daytime look or a super-glam red carpet appearance. And now Taylor's fans can get her glamorous look from her CoverGirl commercials by using the very same makeup Taylor uses everyday!

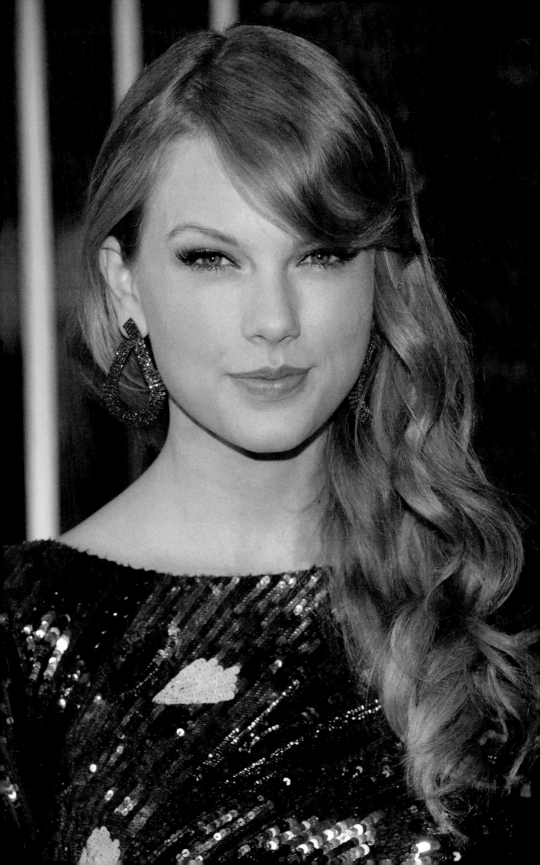

CHAPTER 8
Soundtrack Sensation

While Taylor loves her solo career, she also loves when she's given the opportunity to be a part of a movie soundtrack.

At the start of 2010, Taylor released a new single called "Today Was a Fairytale" for the movie soundtrack of the film *Valentine's Day*. The song debuted at No. 2 on the Billboard Hot 100 chart and broke the record for first-week download sales by a female artist. It was also Taylor's first number-one hit in Canada!

Taylor was especially flattered when she was approached by the producers of *The Hunger Games* movie and asked to create a song for the film's soundtrack. She worked with indie rock duo The Civil Wars to write and record "Safe and Sound," which was released to iTunes on December 23, 2011. It hit number one on the iTunes singles list within twenty-four hours. *The Hunger Games* hit theaters in March 2012 and was a huge smash with fans of the books and fans of Taylor!

The sweet but eerie song was a departure for Taylor and sounds more like independent rock pop than country music. Taylor herself loves the Hunger Games book trilogy, and she

really felt that she captured the feel of the film with her song. Fans of Taylor, the Hunger Games books, and the movie all agree—"Safe and Sound" is a winner!

= CHAPTER 9 =

Sweet Charity

Taylor considers herself very lucky, but
she also knows that not everyone is as lucky
as she is. That's why she has always made a
point to give back to her community and fans.
Early in her career, she was the face of a

Tennessee campaign to help kids stay safe online. She donates money regularly to the Red Cross to help them deal with disasters across the country.

Her relationship with the Red Cross became even more important to Taylor when Nashville was hit with a huge flood in early May 2010. The Red Cross was one of the first organizations to respond to help everyone who had lost their homes.

Taylor was devastated when she realized how badly her adopted hometown had been hit. "It was the craziest thing that I've ever seen . . . It was so heartbreaking to see that in my town, the place that I call home, and the place [where] I feel most safe. I just send my love to my friends and neighbors who got hit harder than I did," Taylor told *Star* magazine. Taylor partnered with the Red Cross and other charities to help her fellow Nashvillians.

Taylor's generosity went a long way toward helping Nashville recover from the flood.

In early 2011, Taylor turned her final dress rehearsal for her *Speak Now* tour into a benefit concert for tornado victims in the southern U.S. Taylor often lends a helping hand to her fans abroad, too! She's donated money to the Australian Red Cross and Children In Need in the UK, as well as playing benefit shows in multiple countries.

Taylor's song "Mean" has become an anthem for kids across America who suffer from bullying. The song was written in response to music critics who give Taylor a hard time, but its "I will prevail" message has given hope to thousands of kids and teens struggling to rise above bullies. No wonder her fans look up to her so much— Taylor really is a hero!

= CHAPTER 10 =
Taylor at Home

Taylor doesn't have a lot of time off, but when she does you can either find her at her loft apartment in Nashville, Tennessee, or in her cottage in Beverly Hills, California. She's had a blast living on her own, especially when it comes to decorating her two homes and whipping up new recipes in the kitchen!

When she's in Nashville, Taylor spends

time with her oldest friend, Abigail, country star Kellie Pickler, and her family. In L.A., Taylor pals around with her best friend and fellow star, Selena Gomez. The two became friends while working at Disney Channel events and have been super close ever since. They love going out for dinner together, catching movies, and having slumber parties where they record funny videos and catch up. They support each other on the road, too—Selena even joined Taylor onstage to perform a duet of Selena's hit song "Who Says" at New York City's Madison Square Garden during Taylor's *Speak Now* tour!

Taylor will be the first to admit that she's obsessed with love, and she's dated her fair share of famous boys including Joe Jonas, Taylor Lautner, and John Mayer. Unfortunately, none of those guys were "the one" for Taylor, but they did inspire some great songs for her albums—

including "Forever and Always," "Back to December," and "Dear John." Taylor is taking a break from boys, but she's still open to finding love. Luckily, she has plenty of time to find her Mr. Right!

So what's next for Taylor? Taylor wants to continue to give her fans and her career one hundred percent of her time and energy. "Even though I am at a place where my dresses are really pretty and the red carpets have a lot of bright lights and I get to play to thousands of people . . . you have to take that with a grain of salt. The stakes are really high if you mess up, if you slack off and don't make a good record, if you make mistakes based on the idea that you are larger than life and you can just coast," Taylor told *Vogue*.

She'd love to continue acting with a few roles and working with great brands like CoverGirl to promote products she knows her

fans will love. Of course, making music will always be her first priority, whether by herself or collaborating with other artists. No matter what Taylor does, her fans know she will continue to wow them and they can't wait to see what she does next!

CHAPTER 11
Taylor Timeline

1989: Born on December 13.

1996: Buys her first LeAnn Rimes album and falls in love with country music.

2002: Learns how to play guitar.

2003: Moves to Nashville area.

2005: Starts attending Hendersonville High School. Writes "Our Song" for freshman year talent show.

2006: Releases her first album, *Taylor Swift*.

2007: Wins CMT "Breakthrough Video of the Year" award.

2008: Releases *Fearless*. Wins "Favorite Female Country Artist" at the American Music Awards.

2009: Kicks off her *Fearless* Tour. Wins the CMAA "Entertainer of the Year" award.

2010: Releases *Speak Now* and stars in the hit movie *Valentine's Day*. Wins four Grammy Awards.

2011: Kicks off her *Speak Now* World Tour. Records the voice of Aubrey in *The Lorax*. Wins multiple awards, including the CMAA "Entertainer of the Year" award for the second time.

2012: Finishes her *Speak Now* World Tour. Releases her fourth album.